MW00809765

The Corporate Jungle

Animal Personalities

Colliding with Job Titles

Rudolf J. Waldner

GOTHAM CITY PUBLISHERS

Welcome

I love wildlife and what has allowed me to experience it more than most is being successful and lucky in business, so it made sense to merge my two passions in this book, "The Corporate Jungle." Using photos I've snapped and snippets from other author's perceptions, combined and sprinkled with my personal observations, I believe that I'll be able to give you a whimsical look at the business world while sharing truths of the animal kingdom and tips on behaviors experienced through different corporate characters lined up by their position in the hierarchy. This writing is all in good fun, so please enjoy it that way.

Little did I realize, but this fixation took root years ago. Growing up I was gifted a book from my godfather, its title was "Safari: A Saga of African Adventure" by Martin Johnson. The book influenced my travel choices markedly, so much so that I've gone on photo safaris all over the planet, and I'm still not done as I need to explore further. Not sure, frankly, that I'll ever shed this Wanderlust.

Dedicated to the fellow travelers along our journey whose glasses I've clicked in a toast or with whom I've waited with on an immigration line, gleefully watching as a new passport stamp was added to our life's story.

Also dedicated to my family, friends & beautiful wife, and most especially to my parents, who've always encouraged travel.

Contents

Map of Countries Highlighted

Zimbabwe, Zambia, Mozambique, South Africa,
Botswana, Canada (Churchill/Manitoba), Kansas,
Missouri, Ecuador with Galapagos, Chile, Argentina,
Costa Rica, Kenya, Tanzania with Zanzibar

Foreword

In the heart of the book you are about to devour, the story of one adventurous life begetting another beats between every line. Author Rudy Waldner's passion for travel was sparked at an early age by explorer Martin Johnson's book "Safari" and this interest has steered Rudy on an amazing life's path.

During a time when most Americans never ventured beyond their own shores, Martin Johnson and his wife Osa brought home the sights – and later sounds – of far-away places that were as wild as they were beautiful. In their films and books, they introduced the public to exotic peoples and presented close-up encounters with epic creatures of lore and legend. The images the Johnsons shined on silver screens across the nation electrified audiences. Many Americans still thought of Africa as the "Dark Continent"– a treacherous, foreboding place. Through their films the Johnsons shattered this common but outdated perspective. Martin and Osa's Africa was a beautiful place, overflowing with amazing landscapes, huge herds of animals and fascinating peoples and it was only momentarily dangerous when they got too near the animals.

As a boy Rudy, like so many generations of young people before him, was transfixed by what Martin Johnson was able to accomplish through hard work and extraordinary marketing prowess. Having been bitten by the travel bug early, Rudy, who today lives in Kansas City, has visited over 55 countries and like Martin Johnson, he has been able to merge his hobby with his professional calling.

After the success of his book "Marketing from the Trenches: Your Guide to Retail Success," Rudy learned that the Martin and Osa Johnson Safari Museum was just two hours from his home. He immediately decided to play his success forward by offering his time and talent to this small nonprofit organization that has a world class collection, but a third world operating budget.

In 2014, in an effort to help publicize the legacy of Martin Johnson, Rudy prepared "The Magic of Africa," a photographic show of his own works for exhibition at the museum. He also donated his time to present a talk and do a book signing at the exhibition launch to further support the museum's educational–driven mission.

As curator of this museum for over 20 years, the best aspect of my job is meeting the fans of Martin and Osa Johnson. I am always astonished at how our titular heroes' story has influenced so many different individuals like Rudy and in so many diverse ways. The reason, perhaps, is that both the Johnsons made concerted efforts to foster global responsibility in their youngest fans. In the midst of WWII, and in the wake Martin's untimely death, Osa made a rousing speech at Rollin's College that was geared specifically to the youth of the world. The closing lines were "Martin and I started with very little schooling and no resources nor help... We had only our hopes and our nerve... Opportunity is something that one has to make for himself, with laborious planning and doing and plenty of suffering. Nothing is impossible, if you want it badly enough, and if you have the imagination to dream and the energy to make your dreams come true."

Those words echoed in my mind the first day I met Rudy and saw how his life trajectory was so clearly guided by the very best that Martin and Osa Johnson offered as role models. I am thrilled to call Rudy, and his own lovely wife Sandra, friends, and can't help but think that Martin and Osa would be so honored to have made such an impression on Rudy's many good life works.

I hope you enjoy this book, but more importantly, I hope that you read it with the spirit of adventure and excitement and enthusiasm that Rudy channeled in it, and that you take away from that experience something that will help guide you on your own path to living up to your own heroes and inspiring others in your own fashion.

Jacquelyn Borgeson Zimmer,
Curator Emeritus (Active)
The Martin and Osa Johnson Safari Museum

Lion:
Chief Operations Officer

Lions truly would be the "Kings of the Jungle", if they lived in jungles, but they do not. Kings, nevertheless they are. They are most assuredly at the top of the food chain, not threatened by any other animal besides man.

Battle scarred for sure, the COO is. He's heard every inventive story concerning child sickness, parent and grandparent deaths, car troubles, pet issues, court ap-

pearances and so on... That's why, just like the resting male lion, you'll find him staring over your head at a place he wishes he was because your sentence started with, "You're not going to believe this, but..." From personal experiences safe inside a safari vehicle and only five feet from a lion, you notice that they'll just ignore you, looking right through you. This speaks to Arrigo Cipriani's comment "Aloof and detached glance of a lion" – from his book "Heloise and Bellinis." Unless he's hungry or his kill or pride is threatened, you're made to feel as significant as a pile of elephant dung.

It's an unnerving experience, being that close to a wild lion. First you tingle with euphoria because you were lucky enough to find a huge male lion, mane blowing in the wind, relaxing on a hilltop or standing over a carcass on a bumpy dirt road. The guide pulls up super close, as your pulse pounds. After the clicking (years ago) and whirring

(present day) of cameras subsides and you actually take in this magnificent creature, you get a sense of the power encased in his dust colored fur. You become a bit surprised and maybe even disappointed as the lion doesn't care about your existence as he peers at the horizon and ever so casually glances at some movement in the distance with his amber eyes.

But, be careful what you hope for because every now and then the huge cat's gaze does seem to lock eyes with

yours. That's when your chest tightens, the hair on your neck stands up, and goose bumps swell up and down your arms. You hold your breath and freeze in whatever position you are in, until, thankfully, he looks away and you realize he wasn't looking at you at all, but rather at the tree-line behind you. You mutter a prayer, even if you don't pray. Peter Capstick's words "crouching death" finally make sense from his book "Death in the Long Grass."

In the corporate jungle, I equate the Lion with a COO or Operations VP. A COO might seem to not be watching, but know that he is. He only acts on relevant issues though, much like his animal kingdom doppelgänger. A COO protects his team, perhaps to a fault, and takes on

the tough battles with clients or other departments. Aside from that he'll gaze over your head because perhaps he's heard the same story one too many times.

Eagle & Hawk:
Chief Executive Officer

Birds of prey are smart, and deadly. Take a look into their cold, black, close-set eyes and you'll feel their unflinching lethal focus. They hunt from a safe distance, rarely if ever putting themselves in harm's way. They swoop in, make the kill, and return back to the safety of their nest way up high away from prying eyes and other carnivores. They sail beautifully in the wind and present a regal profile when you can get close enough to appreciate it.

I've seen birds of prey on four continents and the sight is truly arresting. What a charge it was to experience a predation (fancy word for the preying of one animal on another) in Missouri where a hawk swooped down, clawed a squirrel, and in one motion propelled back up into the sky. Poor squirrel.

I equate birds of prey with CEOs. Most everything is done from a distance. They never really engage with equals without a lawyer (vultures, but that's a different chapter) and as far as subordinates, they never spend much time on the ground – they swoop in, deliver

news and assignments, or swing the sickle, then take off back to their crow's nest to appreciate the view of their kingdom. From that vantage point they continue to survey their fiefdoms and speculate about expanding their influence or area. Be careful not to stand too close as you're liable to be splashed with Gin from their martini glass from on high, should they encounter any sort of turbulence.

Wild Dog:
Sales Manager

Wild Dogs are unique is so many ways. Attractive to look at, yet deadly. Unlike what I would have guessed, they can't crossbreed with domestic dogs, even though wolves and coyotes can. They are run by a matriarch and travel, hunt, and live in packs. I've encountered these predators all over Africa.

In South Africa we came upon a small group of five Wild Dogs that had just taken down a wildebeest. Their snouts and most of their faces were covered in blood. The remains of the animal were being literally torn apart. Cartlidge popped, tendons snapped, muscles and flesh and skin ripped, and bones crunched. A ritualistic blood bath it was. Liquid red was splattered and dripped all over the high grass. Everywhere. The incessant crunching made hair on the back on my neck and arms stand up. I will never forget the sound of bones being crushed by the jaws of these killers.

The first pack of Wild Dogs I experienced was in Zambia near a remote camp in South Luangwa National Park. We were traveling at top speed in a safari jeep

towards an airstrip to catch a bush flight. Suddenly we were surrounded by yelping dogs that jumped as high as the hood of the Toyota Land Cruiser. At least five feet high, it seemed. It became clear that we'd injected ourselves into the middle of a hunt.

A dog in the rear yelped what sounded like orders while the other leaping dogs on the flanks reported back with barks, charging forward. A terrified impala was smashing through and over the undergrowth. The u-shaped pack

engulfed the impala as we sped away. I'm not upset that I missed the takedown.

Wild dogs are Sales Managers in the corporate world. They often partake in, or lead a crazy pulse-pounding ritual before the day begins to hit sales goals, which is mimicked by packs of wild dogs as they get psyched up for a hunt. A quote from Hugo and Jane van Lawick-Goodall's book "Innocent Killers" drives home the frantic sales team analogy. I've condensed their passage to hone in on

my point. "Their squeaks gradually changed to frenzied twittering. In a moment all the adult dogs joined them and soon the pack was swirling round and round in the greeting ceremony. The wild flurry of activity subsided and the pack started to trot away on its evening hunt. This ceremony nearly always takes place before a pack sets off hunting." Sounds like a pre-shift sales huddle to me!

Hyena:
Government Regulator

Hyenas are fierce predators. Up close it's easy to confirm that they are built for relentless aggression. They are front heavy with shoulders and necks that look disproportionately large compared to the rest of their stature, bulging with muscles that propel their glistening teeth and powerful jaws towards any flesh within range. I shuddered when I got close to one in Zambia. Their look conveys nothing but menace.

In Botswana, while traveling with a tented safari, we were told of an incident that kept us up all night. The dancing light of our campfire cast creepy shadows behind us, toying with our peripheral vision, suggesting all sorts of scary possibilities. The clear, cold and black sky was dotted with bright white stars that didn't do much for lighting though beautiful to behold. We leaned into the campfire to allow the heat from the flames to join in with the gin; one heating us from the inside the other from the outside. A fellow traveler hailing from Russia, Michael, mentioned to our  guide that he'd Googled our safari route and read about a teenager being killed and eaten by a pack of hyenas. Our

guide Nick dropped his head but kept eye contact, scanning the group. Slowly and reluctantly he shared with us that at the neighboring camp, a few hundred yards away, is where the slaughter had occurred. A mother was traveling with her teenage son and wanted to give him his personal space so he had claimed his own tent. Apparently, he'd not secured the tent flap and was dragged out and devoured by a team of Hyenas. I managed to pour a triple gin & tonic as we all sat in silence for a bit.

I believe the human counterparts to Hyenas are government regulators. They attack relentlessly until there's a corpse or something similar to show for their efforts. By corpse I might be implying a tax bill or a fine. A quote from Karl Lenker's "Final Trumpet" (an action-packed tale of Africa) sums it up from my perspective. "Those that can, do. Those that can't do, teach. Those who can't teach become critics. And those that can do none of the above, regulate."

Described as a lethal killer in the wild, the same goes for the hyena's counterpart. Once a regulator has you in his sights, you're either dead (out of business) or maimed (severely fined).

Iguana:
The Maintenance Guy

Maintenance personnel don't seem to have a sense of urgency, until maybe lunchtime. Piles of stock items often lay unassembled and scattered throughout corners, shelves, and storage areas. "Maintenance" is only in the job title, it's more like "react to an emergency and remain scarce in-between."

I've enjoyed spotting Iguana all over Central and South America. On the Galapagos many were clustered and just hanging out. Others were meandering, not very quickly, and basically enjoying life at their own pace, just like the maintenance workers.

Jackal:
Friend of Owner

In their book "Innocent Killers", jackals are described by Hugo and Jane van Lawick-Goodall as "daring scavengers." That sums it up. Jackals are adorable to observe. They are super protective of their families and playful when the time is right. They always seem to be scanning their surroundings, probably seeking opportunity as well as sustaining security. I was lucky enough to stumble across a family of jackals in Tanzania and also a pair in Botswana.

In the wild these animals are a fun and lively part of the ecosystem, so please do not let my description of their corporate counterparts taint your opinion of these furry rascals. Jackals are scavengers, so, they rely on other's work. They are very fast so they nip and get away at lightning speed to avoid retaliation.

I call them F.O.O.s (pronounced foes). In the corporate world these creatures are rampant. Ask any employee anywhere, who are the "Friends Of the Owner?" This network of snitches usually produce subpar work, are the laziest of employees, but are afforded the full protection of the owner with tenure more solid than a college professor's. These are the luckiest of all employees as they don't have to earn their keep. They point fingers and criticize with no ramifications yet produce nothing of substance. And of course, once they fully realize their situation, they exploit it.

In the wild, this relationship actually exists between the Lion and the Jackal. The jackal keeps a lookout and in trade, the Lion allows the jackal some scraps. The corporate version is much less palatable.

Polar Bear:
Collections Manager

Polar Bears are the unchallenged Lords of the Arctic. Fortunately I saw a few of these surprisingly cute yet powerful and dangerous animals in Churchill, Canada. Some were lounging on snow banks, simply enjoying the

blizzard conditions. They'd stretch out and allow the snow to cover them in a most tranquil way, like you and I might stretch out on a sunny beach with the waves lapping in time to Mother Nature's pulse.

I also witnessed a large Polar Bear sauntering through a barking pack of sled dogs without even noticing them. Now that's confidence. Dozens of dogs snarling, yelping, and growling; yet the Prince of the North just walked straight through the pack. Master of his domain, for sure. In the wild, Polar Bears are truly, as Glenn Hopfner describes in his book "Tales from the Tundra," Lords of the Arctic.

In the corporate world I equate the Polar Bear with a Collections or Loss Prevention Manager. They walk with quite the swagger. This is an elite group of individuals that keep to themselves (solitary just like Polar Bears). While they respect each other they are obsessively territorial – each having their own secret formula for success. And I used the word swagger deliberately.

They saunter through companies with great confidence and poise. My guess is that all their self-assurance comes from turning bad debt into a profit center for most any company they work for. Once you have the CFO's or CEO's ear, your standing on pretty solid ground, able to throw down with just about anybody or any department. And just like their wild counterparts, they only run or

spring into action when attacked or attacking. But their usual personality is that of royalty, nonchalantly observing their domain.

Two-Toed Sloth:
Night Manager

The two-toed sloth is nocturnal, slow moving, not easy to look at, and quite the loner. He hangs out on hard to reach branches at the tops of trees.

Click over to a business environment and the two-toed sloth, or as they're called in Spanish, the "lazy bear," definitely describes an overnight supervisor. Night managers are inherently nocturnal and I wouldn't describe them as quick. They have quirky communication skills, enjoy the slow pace and demands of overnight shifts, and seem out of place in daylight.

Monkey: Trainee

Monkeys and baboons are so much fun to watch because they emulate human movements. And they are brats. I was sleeping in a tin roofed hut in Zambia when I was awakened by the constant clatter of seeds being thrown at my ceiling. I swear that laughing monkey was so happy to wake me early in the morning. He'd obviously done this to previous guests and loved the reaction his actions caused.

Once while on Safari in Zambia, our truck got stuck in the mud of a river bed. As we were digging, shoveling, and struggling to free the axles, a troop of baboons came quite close to our right flank. On the left, a parade of elephants got closer as well. It was an interesting phenomenon as we got caught up in our work, these two wild but organized sets of families somehow sharing the same space with us. It was like grabbing a spot on the beach or putting a blanket down in a park. As the day progressed, more and more people (in this case, animals) occupied the area.

Like Martin Johnson wrote in "Safari," "Baboons are the most entertaining of all the animals we know, because they are grotesquely like human beings." Meaning, they are eerily similar to us.

❧

On the corporate side of things, I feel that monkeys (baboons are a type of monkey) are like trainees. They try and mimic our actions almost to a fault. We often see ourselves in trainees by sometimes watching them make the same mistakes that we've made.

❧

Giraffe:
Human Resources

Giraffes parade with a dignity that makes them the gentry of the African plains. In Tanzania's Serengeti National Park, we observed the largest kaleidoscope of Giraffe that our guides – as well as ourselves – had ever seen. Magnificent. All the regal visuals of what the Habsburg court must have looked like while Mozart performed his first arrangement hoping to get their nod of approval.

It is thought that a giraffe's pattern resembles tree leaves. Makes sense as they're always eating from tree tops as their long necks blend in, resembling a tree trunk. This camouflages them, somewhat, from predators.

In Botswana I saw what I thought was two giraffes

playing a game, or performing a mating ritual. The adult giraffes were twisting their necks in ever-so-slow circular movements. Our guide informed us that it was actually two males fighting.

Giraffes and HR personnel share the same genes. Jumping to the corporate jungle – have you ever, ever, and I mean ever, gotten anything from an HR department in a reasonable amount of time and without having to follow-up? I can't make this up, my wife has some funds left in a previous employer's 401K. It has literally been seven years since she's drawn a paycheck from that asylum.

Usually though, most HR leadership has a grace and poise emulated by few, just like the giraffe.

Leopard: Entrepreneur

In Peter Capstick's book "Death in the Long Grass" he describes the leopard as one of the most powerful, elusive, clever, bold, and dangerous animals in the world today. The leopard is able to carry prey weighing three times it's bodyweight up a tree to protect it from other predators. It is not infrequent that a lion pride would steal a leopard's freshly caught meal. In Tanzania we saw a mother leopard greet her two teenage offspring in a family reunion of sorts. A majestic animal for sure.

The Leopard's success is evident by its presence from South Africa to China. No other predator besides man has that large a territory. This is possible by its adaptability. From icy mountains to steaming swamps, the Leopard thrives. The only adversary he can't overcome is man's encroachment.

So here's the way I see it. Lions are stronger than Leopards and work together (like lobbyists along with corporate America, legally bribing government) but – leopards (sole proprietors) work alone and still function quite successfully in areas controlled by a strong force like a pride of Lions. They are adaptable. They find a way to successfully thrive with fierce competition using their speed and cunning. The "Trench Marketers" of the animal world without a doubt.

Buffalo: Debtors

"They (Cape Buffalo) look at you as if they owe you money." ~Peter Capstick, "Death in the Long Grass"

See my photos, stare them right in the eyes, and you'll see what makes this statement so profound.

I've observed huge armies of more than three hundred

strong in Botswana's Okavango delta as well as single beasts wandering, usually old males rejected from the group.

One of these shunned males dined right outside my tent along the Zambezi on the Zambian side, keeping me awake, frightened and sweating all night. Hiding under the sheets just didn't do the trick. Imagine a piece of canvas between you and who-knew-what-at-the-time,

literally three feet away: chomping, slobbering, grinding, and huffing loudly. When it became necessary to use the bathroom (number one) and believe me I held it till I turned yellow, I actually relieved myself into a pitcher of water and four serving glasses as there was no way that I would open the tent flap.

As I travel the globe, there are events that make me ask (think of the line by the Talking Heads), "How did I get here?" Usually, it happens when I'm scared beyond belief. But after each harrowing or challenging situation, I find that I've lived another most memorable instance in my life.

〜

Water Buffalo usually congregate in herds and defend against attacks by standing shoulder to shoulder and charging when needed. On the human side, they remind me of a Debtor.

When trying to collect a debt you get the same look or blocking tactics from the rest of the group or family.

I've included photos of American Bison, usually inaccurately referred to as buffalo. I was able to get up-close-and-personal to two herds of American Bison, one in Kansas and one in Colorado.

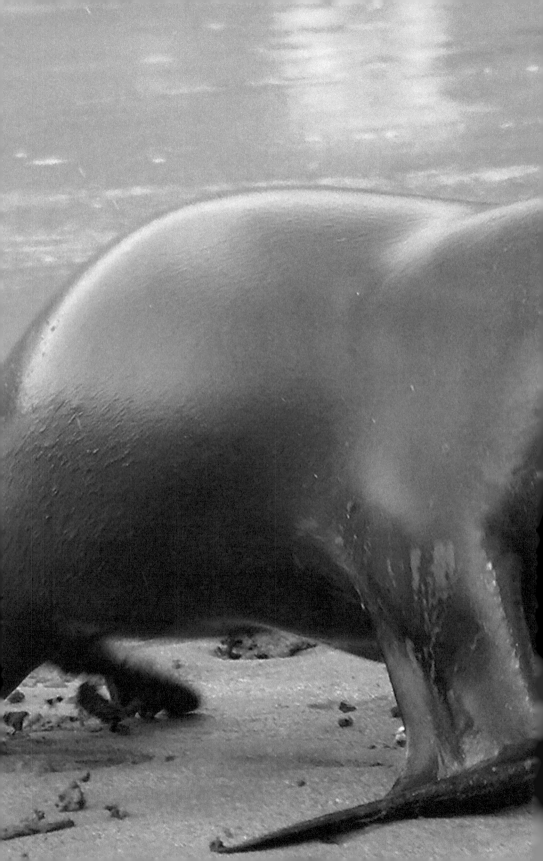

Seal & Sea Lion:
Compliance Administrator

A colony of sea lions or seals is a noisy group of individual animals, barking and playfully nudging and nipping. All in all, a pod is a fun-loving group, banded together to socialize and to survive.

I've been aboard a dive boat near Seal Island, off of Gansbaai, South Africa, which is home to over 60,000 Cape Fur Seals. Not to depress you, but we did a Great White Shark dive and the Fur Seal colony was the "draw," or bait, as it were.

On a lighter note, while visiting the Galapagos, which is near and a part of Ecuador, we had the privilege of sunbathing with these friendly animals. They know they have the run of the islands. They'll not move out of the way for you. They'll even take your spot on the beach –which  is exactly what they did to us. We went for a dip in the Pacific; when we returned, sprawled comfortably and permanently on our blankets was a small clique of these adorable creatures.

The corporate jungle's version is a bit more cynical. Compliance Administrators are loud and tend to bark like seals. They attempt to make a name for themselves by publicizing the mistakes of others. Like their animal counterparts, they band together for protection, as being the perpetual antagonist paints a target on one's back.

Elephant:
Board of Directors Member

Ah. . . the elephant, one of my favorite animals on the globe. In "The Garden of Eden," Hemingway describes the elephant as dignified, majestic, and beautiful. I'm in total agreement.

During a rare foot safari in Zambia, our group stumbled directly into a parade of elephants. It's hard to convey how insignificant and vulnerable one feels while standing on the ground, gazing up at these huge creatures. It's an entirely different perspective from the view while sitting in a jeep (and don't get me started about zoos). We were as startled as they were. The lead elephant flapped her enormous ears in alarm, but did not trumpet or charge. Both groups froze for a moment, and then our askari yelled "run." Of course I said, "But you said never run in Africa." He responded with a scowl. As our guide had the only rifle, I stayed right next to him as the tourists sprinted back towards our safari jeep. The guide and I stood between the elephants and the scampering crew. In the end the elephants made a sharp left, as did we, sending us in opposite directions. What. A. Rush.

In his novel "Final Trumpet," Karl Lenker describes elephants as the undisputed rulers of the water hole. They

dominate all who come to drink or bathe. Karl goes on to give the elephants credit for creating many of the ponds so it is only fair that they have something to say about it.

In Botswana I watched as two hyenas squared off with a large bull elephant. The bull trumpeted and made a few faux charges which eventually scared the hyenas off.

Switching over to the corporate jungle, who controls the currency, the "water?" Clearly, it's the board of directors. They control entry onto the board, and when you're

on, you receive help in all sorts of ways that the common-
er does not. Children of board members are afforded an
education and access available to only the chosen few.

Crocodile & Alligator:
Chief Financial Officer

This was the first correlation I thought of when I was first concepting "The Corporate Jungle." It was too easy, a CFO snaps "no" before a budgetary question is even completed.

In the wild, these prehistoric predators are lethal to humans. As Capstick writes in his book "Maneaters," crocodiles are land's only carnivores that will cheerfully kill and eat you every time he gets the chance." In other words, most predators can be coerced to look elsewhere for food, but not the crocodile. So here's the segue to the corporate behavior of a CFO.

They are brutally consistent, eager to trim body count to make the columns add up and to pump the brakes on anything that they're not on the receiving end of.

As a point of interest crocodiles have a more narrow snout than the alligator. They also have their fourth tooth menacingly showing while their jaws are shut.

Zebra:
Operations Manager

I love zebras as I believe their playful (forgive this) horsing around resembles that of an operations team. In front of customers or clients they are all usually good natured but behind the scenes like in the break room or at an afterhours function, there is relentless playful banter. Martin Johnson, in his book "Africa" describes zebras as silly, rowdy, and roaming in big herds. These beautiful animals can be seen all over Africa. Sometimes they travel in single file which is a delight to behold.

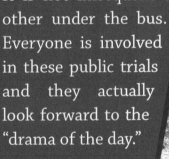

Like operators, Zebras are always messing around. When two zebras have a quarrel, others snap and kick, sort of spurring on the behavior – just like in operations. It is not infrequent that one operator will throw another under the bus. Everyone is involved in these public trials and they actually look forward to the "drama of the day."

Hippo:
Account Executive

The hippopotamus is the most dangerous animal on the planet accounting for more human deaths annually than any other beast, according to Peter Capstick.

After a sleepless night in a safari camp which included a noisy Cape Buffalo outside of my tent, I scheduled what I thought would be a calming canoe trip down the Zambezi River.

The guide greeted me with a tanned face and a big smile. A seasoned bush and river guide, he pushed off from shore and commandeered the lead canoe. I had a young intern muscling my dugout forward as I snapped pictures of both the Zimbabwe and Zambia shores. The Zambezi River forms part of a natural border between Zambia and Zimbabwe. In the border towns of

Livingstone and Victoria Falls, this area is known as the "Zim-Zam" border.

Cape Buffalo were plentiful on the shores as were the nostrils of curious Hippo on the surface of the river, snorting and huffing, and staring at us from glassy, dull pink-rimmed eyes. Their entire 2000-pound masses were submerged. Contrary to popular belief, their bulky appearance isn't because of fat, but of muscle. And they're not slow either; on land they can reach up to 30 miles per hour.

Bird calls, a brilliant morning sun, and the gentle dip of paddles into the water made for a relaxing sojourn, or at least that's how it seemed...

We drifted down a narrow branch of the river where the reeds hugged the waterway. The current sped up a bit, and suddenly there she was: a huge Hippo up to her shoulders in water, on the riverbank. Did I mention that Hippos are territorial, and that most charges are incited by someone or something crossing in to what they perceive to be their territory?

This huge gray boulder-like mass began snorting and trembling as we drifted closer, creating quite a commotion. The bird calls were silenced, replaced by the throbbing of my pulse. We couldn't slow our progress against the current, let alone change directions. As I said before, the channel was narrow, and it was getting narrower.

The rest happened so quickly that I like to replay it over and over again in my mind, relishing every detail of this heart-pounding and most memorable episode of my life. As we drifted closer and eventually perpendicular to where she stood on the shore, the hippo let out a roar that set the hair on my neck on end. Two huge ivory tusks glistened in the sun and phlegm and water sprayed side to side as she opened her pink maw and shook her monstrous head. Another clutch-your-chest roar and more splattering phlegm, and she lurched forward. Water parted before her charge like the Red Sea's parting before Charlton Heston's staff.

I managed to click away as my canoe partner paddled furiously like a cartoon character. Roddy, the guide, raised his paddle and slapped the water's surface with the flat side of his oar. As his oar hit the surface it let out a crack like that of a gunshot. Thank god. The agitated wa-ter monster stopped in her tracks. Again, thank Buddha.

We kept drifting and let out nervous laughs as we got out of range. Further down the river I had some choice words that I'll not print here, but the first word of the two-word phrase started with "Holy."

From that day on, and still to this day, I truly believe that was the best experience I've had in my entire life-time. Why is it, do you think, that the closer we get to death, the more alive we feel?

Flipping over to a corporate comparison, the hippo most reminds me of an Account Executive. Loud and always charging at something or somebody for dramatic effect and attention. Right-hand to the CEO or owner because of their salary and the nature of their work, they feel empowered to treat other departments in a cavalier manner. Think FOO (Friend of Owner), but with a higher salary. From Capstick's "Death in the Long Grass": "Tourists love to take pictures of hippos displaying their big yawns. What they're actually doing is showing you what they

have to work with, their tusks. This is a form of saber rattling." Think about who else might have the car matching the bosses? This is boastful and saber rattling of a different nature. In addition to being haughty, they're louder than most.

In short, Account Executives are flashy and empowered beyond their station. Referencing how dangerous the hippo is in the wild, as mentioned before, the AE is as dangerous in the corporate world. If you're on the bad side of an AE, because the Account Executive has the boss's ear, you're apt to get fired quicker than if you stole money or slept with the boss's daughter.

〜

Warthog:
Customer Service Representative

Warthogs are so fun to watch and listen to. They grunt and snuffle while eating, leaning on their front "elbows" digging through topsoil with their tusks and snouts in search of grass, roots, and bugs to nosh on. They parade across savannas with their tails high in the air like stiff antennas at a trot similar to that of a quarter horse.

During a visit to Victoria Falls, using an inaccurate tourist map, I cut across a field thinking I was closer to the town center than I was. The grass was high as I came upon a still smoking hot pile of droppings. I turned around and got back to the road. Things didn't feel right. As I stepped onto the gravel, on the other side stood a male warthog. Thankful that it wasn't a more dangerous predator but still alarmed because of a story I remembered from one of Capstick's books about a warthog ripping off the knee cap of an innocent bystander, I froze. We eyed each other for a bit and then he trotted away. Thank goodness. Though a full grown male is only three feet tall, he does weigh up to 330 pounds and his tusks grow as long as 25 inches.

Warthogs represent CSRs in corporate life. They're mostly good natured and always interesting to watch in action.

Vulture: Lawyer

Throughout literature and over the years I read in almost every genre about the "smell of death." Though I appreciated the prose, I never really understood what was meant by the phrase "the smell of death," until my last trip to the Serengeti. On the Kenya/Tanzania border, our safari jeep drove up to a committee of vultures fighting and picking over a carcass. Well before we got within 30 feet of the heaving pile of wings and beaks and claws, an unseen cloud of an overwhelming fetor enveloped us – yes – the proverbial "smell of death." It was

as if the breeze slapped you in the face with this heavy, nose-stinging stench. I couldn't wait to shower and wash my clothes.

❧

In a less dramatic encounter on Papagayo Bay on the west coast of Costa Rica, I was able to walk up rather close to some buzzards in the process of gutting a dead fish's belly, which lends itself nicely to the comparison between a vulture and a lawyer.

I think it's so easy to align these two, the vulture and the lawyer, because it does seem that whenever I've dealt with a lawyer, I've been on the losing end. No matter the outcome of a case, the lawyer gets paid, and someone is left behind, gutted!

Conclusion

I hope that you've enjoyed my perspective of both the animal kingdom and the corporate jungle, because to be sure, it is a jungle. Survival of the fittest is always at play, even if it's disguised by political correctness.

Observing animals in their natural habitat, to me, is one of the most rewarding experiences available to us. I very much hope that you've enjoyed a taste of that through my camera's lens and my campfire stories. And know that you needn't travel to faraway places for similar encounters, sometimes a nearby park offers similar treasures.

Lodges, Parks, Ships, Camps, and **Museums** that have opened a brave new world to me, many of which these photos were taken at or near:

Mfuwe Lodge and one of their Bushcamps
Mpika, Zambia
Phone: +260 21 6246041

Madikwe Safari Lodge
Madikwe Game Reserve, Madikwe, 0116, South Africa
Phone: +27 18 350 9902

Klein's Camp
Serengeti, Tanzania
Phone: +255 28 262 1629

andBeyond Serengeti Under Canvas
Serengeti, Serengeti National Park (mobile camp), Tanzania

Maxwell Wildlife Refuge
Off of Highway 86, Canton, Kansas, USA

Squaw Creek National Wildlife Refuge
Five miles South of Mound City, Missouri, USA

Lazy Bear Lodge
313 Kelsey Blvd, Churchill MB R0B 0E0, Canada
Phone: +1 204-663-9377

Tortuga Lodge & Gardens
Across from the airstrip, 1 mile north of the Town of Tortuguero, Tortuguero, Costa Rica, 6941

Le Cameleon Boutique Hotel
Cocles Beach Puerto Viejo, Limon, Costa Rica
Phone: +506 2750 0501

Galapagos Legend Cruise Ship
Ecuador
Phone: +1-403-760-3565 Fax: +1-403-760-3566

Royal Livingstone Hotel
Mosi-Oa-Tunya Rd, Livingstone, Zambia
Phone: 021 3321122

Victoria Falls Hotel
1 Mallet Drive, Victoria Falls, Matabeleland North, PO
Box 10, Zimbabwe
Phone: +263 13 44751

Alpasion Lodge & Vineyards
Ruta Proviancial 94 s/n M5560 Tunuyan, Argentina
Phone: +54 9 261 625-9393

Hotel Boutique Casadoca
Av Borgoño 22090, 2510000, Concón, Chile

Martin and Osa Johnson Safari Museum
111 N Lincoln Ave, Chanute, KS 66720, USA
Phone: (620) 431-2730

Wild Earth Llama Adventures
Taos, New Mexico
www.LlamaAdventures.com
Phone: 800-758-5262

Bibliography

Brower, Charles D. *Fifty Years below Zero: A Lifetime of Adventure in the Far North*. New York: Dodd, Mead, 1942. Print.

Capstick, Peter Hathaway. *Death in the Long Grass*. New York: St. Martin's, 1977. Print.

Capstick, Peter Hathaway. *Death in the Silent Places*. New York: St. Martin's, 1981. Print.

Capstick, Peter Hathaway. *Maneaters*. Los Angeles, CA: Petersen Pub., 1981. Print.

Cipriani, Arrigo. *Heloise and Bellinis: A Novel*. New York: Arcade Pub., 1991. Print.

Corbett, Jim. *Man-eaters of Kumaon*. New York: Oxford UP, 1946. Print.

Corbett, Jim. *The Temple Tiger*. Bombay: Oxford UP, 1988. Print.

Hemingway, Ernest, and Robert W. Lewis. *Under Kilimanjaro*. Kent, OH: Kent State UP, 2005. Print.

Hemingway, Ernest. *The Garden of Eden*. New York: C. Scribner's, 1986. Print.

Hemingway, Ernest. *Green Hills of Africa*. New York: Perma, 1954. Print.

Hopfner, Glenn. *Tales from the Tundra*. Ste. Rose, MB: Glenn Hopfner, 2005. Print.

Johnson, Martin. *Safari: A Saga of African Adventure*. New York: Grosset and Dunlap, 1928. Print.

Lawick, Hugo Van, and Jane Goodall. *Innocent Killers*: Ill. with Photographs. Boston: Mifflin, 1971. Print.

Lenker, Karl. "Final Trumpet Hardcover – January 15, 2008."

Marciano, Francesca. *Rules of the Wild*. New York: Pantheon, 1998. Print.

Peacock, Doug. *Grizzly Years: In Search of the American Wilderness*. New York: H. Holt, 1990. Print.

"What Are Groups of African Animals Called? - Africa Freak Blog." Africa Freak Blog. N.p., n.d. Web. 12 Nov. 2015.

CPSIA information can be obtained
at www.ICGtesting.com
Printed in the USA
BVHW091040051120
592530BV00016B/96/J